Has My Soul Been SOLD? by Dr. Marlene Miles

Freshwater Press 2024

freshwaterpress9@gmail.com

ISBN: 978-1-963164-60-2

Paperback Version

Table of Contents

Has

My

Soul

Been

SOLD?

Freshwater

Be Made Whole

God begat Jesus; but God doesn't just want one son; God wants many sons. When God created us, He created us and said, It is good. And God created man perfect and whole. When we receive salvation, we are then authorized to become sons of God. So after salvation the rest of our process is to *become*.

In that *becoming* we must remain a whole soul and prosper in our souls. In the process of reaching soul prosperity, the enemy throws every trick that he can at a soul to keep him from maturing and attaining to the things of God. One of the things the enemy does is to introduce interlopers into a person's soul to interfere with the process and even take that soul over, if at all possible.

One cannot become a whole soul until he expels strangers (strange *gods* from his soul) that is deliverance, resistance, maintenance, *becoming* – living and finishing the work.

If you are a serious student, you cannot finish your coursework and earn your degree, that is, matriculate until you get those party loving, frat boy roommates out of your dorm room so you can focus and study. Strangers in your soul are like frat boys on a serious college campus. These strangers are idol *gods* and even though they are not playing with you, they want to distract you, and entice you to play, fool around, goof off, party, have fun, and sin. Once you sin, the trap is sprung.

We are responsible for making our souls prosper. We should prosper more each day reaching to the image of God.

Loss of Humanity

Loss of your soul or any part of it will manifest as a loss of humanity. So, you've lost part of your humanity by locking it away, by not exposing it to the love and the Spirit of God it is usually because your soul, or some part of it is captive and cannot respond as it should. Your soul cannot respond as Jesus would.

If God cannot identify you as human, 100% human there is no way you can become a son of God.

You lost part of your humanity, by sinning, by works of the flesh. When your responses in life are the opposite of Love, the opposite of what Jesus would do, then the human part of yourself is diminished. Sin chips away at your humanity. So, if the devil can't get you all at once, he'll be happy with bit by bit, chip by chip. If your humanity is diminished, God cannot identify you, people cannot identify you as human and relate to you properly, or at all.

Because you want to stay jealous, you choose to stay hurt, you would rather stay in unforgiveness or you think it makes you look strong and not weak to stay in bitterness, this allows the devil entrance to take pieces of your humanity away until you are diminished, or you're all the way used up, all the way gone. Your humanity is expressed through your soul.

Souls are diluted when clouded with idols. *Idols* won't get into Heaven, so any hybrid of human plus idol is not acceptable either; it is synthetic. We have to be all human, the way God made us--, only more prospered, soul wise.

You've heard people say, I don't think he's *all there*. Well, maybe he's not. Maybe parts of his humanity have been lost or locked away and he could still be just walking around looking alive, appearing to be alive, but maybe he's a soulless zombie or he is spiritually dead.

Don't you be the person who has become evil and hateful or cold and uncaring because of losing the warm and compassionate part of your soul. You may not even know that it is gone or has been locked away. Once the devil has control over your soul, it's *lights out* for you and your humanity. *Lights out* is still a soul death knell whether its on a dimmer switch for you, rather than the entire light bulb suddenly blowing all at once.

If you've closed yourself off from the Spirit of God there's no way to get those lost parts of your humanity back, except by God and the Spirit of Deliverance. **HE RESTORES MY SOUL. That's what that means.**

Any time you close any part of your humanity off from God, you've allowed the devil in. And then the devil took, perverted, or ruined whatever he could steal, kill, destroy, or devour, step by step. If not all at once, part by part, piece by piece. Most of the time it is so subtle that you don't even realize that anything is happening.

It's like putting together a 2000-piece jigsaw puzzle and not realizing that three or four pieces are missing until the very end. If you don't have all the pieces of a jigsaw puzzle it will never achieve its right *form* or image. You could have been so relaxed putting that puzzle together until you got to the end and were shocked that you couldn't finish the work.

Don't let that be your life. Don't be so busy moving the pieces of your life around until you find out at the end that you cannot achieve the image and the likeness of the One who sent you because vital pieces are missing. Don't wait too late to find that those pieces have been stolen or destroyed.

The Word says to possess your soul, your whole soul, not just some of it. That means that all of your soul should be under subjection of your spirit man, which should be under auspices of the Holy Spirit of God. That is the correct form to aspire to, with no voids. Like butter in those thousand little pores in an

English muffin, demons will come to situate themselves in any void in your soul. Therefore, the goal is to be totally filled up by the Holy Spirit so there are no voids, so there are no vacant spaces that idol *gods*, demons, or devils can squat in.

The serpent in the Garden was described as subtle. Was this erosion of your soul subtle? Did you even notice? Please know that locking off parts of your humanity is by your agreement and your own decision, such as when you refuse to forgive, for example. Or, if you choose to hate another or another people group. Racism is soul captivity, folks.

When people lose their humanity, they may become robotic, zombie-like, Stepford spouses-- just going through the motions, just going through life, doing what everyone else is doing--, what *people* are doing, and not what God is doing. Your soul is the very thing that makes you totally unique, goes missing or when it's damaged, when it's foreshortened, it's as though you lose your identity. A person could become apathetic, sad, depressed. A person could be the happiest frat boy on campus and never know that his soul has been compromised, captive--, at least, at first.

The Word of God says we are to possess our souls in sanctification and honor. We are to prosper our souls.

Beloved, I wish above all things you would prosper and be in health even as your soul prospers.(3 John 2)

God would not have told us to *possess* our souls unless there was going to be an issue, a challenge, or some type of attack regarding possessing our own souls. When you send your kid off to school or college and you give them certain valuable possessions, do you not tell them once again to be sure to come back home with that item or items? Of course, you do.

Possess ye your souls.

Whatever you used to sin with, that's what and where the devil can access to attack you and perhaps even destroy that thing. Whether personal sin, ancestral and generational sin, or even full-blown evil dedication, sin has been rampant and organized in a bloodline for so many generations that the devil has full access to that whole family.

Whatever body part you sinned with, or you used to sin with, you grant the devil access to that part of your body, that part of your soul, that part of your spirit, and your life.

So, you wake up from some crazy dream one morning, be it a one-time dream, or a repetitive dream, you better find out what that dream means because is that God trying to tell you something?

Probably.

If not, is the devil trying to attack you?

Either way, you need to know the proper interpretation, so you know how to pray. Dreams are not night videos, night mini-series, or telenovelas. They are not just so you have something to talk about with your friends. *I had this crazy dream.* No, you have got work to do. And in doing that work you are acknowledging that there is a spirit world, and that you know about it and are a part of it. Ultimately, you are acknowledging that you are a spirit, and that is essential knowledge to perfecting your *becoming a son of God--*, completing the work regarding your *becoming*.

Speak the Word of God, against any evil dream and tell the devil what he's going to do and what he's not going to do as it pertains to you, your family, and the people for whom you pray. You speak, you give voice to the Word of God, resist the devil and he will flee from you.

When you're asleep, you may be in severe warfare. You might have a Word problem, that would be if you're not studying the Word, reading and getting the Word in you, and building up your spirit man. **That** is a Word problem. Spiritual warfare works best if you have the Word in you.

You can't just be floating through life thinking, *Ohh, I'm saved*. This is not a cartoon; this is your real life. And you think you're just going to live a life of leisure and living what you call your best life. Well, spiritually thinking that, hey, since you accepted Jesus, you got baptized, you have anything else to do? Yeah, you do. You have lots more to do because the devil does not respect you.

Many people don't even believe he exists. He's got a battering ram, trying to break down the doors of your house, the gates of your city, the walls of your life. Your fortified towns, your man-made fortifications that make you think you're secure, but suddenly you're going to learn today that if you think he doesn't exist, you will either fight no one spiritually, or you will take it into the physical realm and fight PEOPLE--, flesh and blood, and that is a strict no-no.

The devil doesn't respect you. Your walls, your doors, your boundaries, or your fortresses. You have to enforce your boundaries when it comes to the devil. Fortresses that are not of God, if they're not watched over spiritually with divine support, they that watch will watch in vain. Except the Lord build the house, they that labor, labor in vain.

The devil takes advantage of every access point to get into your life, soul, and body that he can; if you think he doesn't, you're living in a fool's paradise.

Personal sin allows the devil in. Unless we are repenting, man usually runs from or hides from God when he sins. Blocking any part of yourself or your life from God shuts that part of your life down.

Stop shutting down parts of your soul. Your intellect, your mind, is a part of your soul. Stop shutting down parts of your humanity. Don't shut down your intellect. Don't say that you will never read a book again because you graduated from high school. Shutting down any part of yourself stagnates your life and stifles the growth and development of your God-intended *form*.

Just because God breathed life into the first man, Adam, and he became a living soul, a human being, the devil's going to come for mankind. Don't make it easy for him by shutting down parts of yourself from God. You need to give God access to all of yourself.

Love the Lord with all of your being and allow God to love ALL of you.

Love the Lord. Your God with all your heart. And with all your soul, and with all your mind, and with all your strength, (Matthew 12:30).

The devil is after you all day, all night, even in your dreams. You dream in symbols for the most part. The following are dream examples of a soul being in trouble. The message is given in the dream, but the soul is in trouble spiritually and in reality. That soul could be captive, being hunted, locked up, stolen, or sold. Dreams of being lost, trapped, wandering, chased, or attacked by animals, or by people are all troubling dreams if you know anything spiritually. If you just think you ate the wrong thing, ate too late at night, or watched a violent movie, or you just love animals and they are cute, you will let this go by and the devil can do anything he wants to you sooner, or later. Animals should not be in your dreams. Period.

You have to find out what all your dreams mean. Sex in the dream. Marrying people in the dream. Marrying people you know. Marrying people you don't know. Marrying strangers. Dreaming of dead people. Some are masquerades; these are all tricks of the enemy.

Signing documents in a dream. Eating food in a dream. Getting injections in a dream. These are horrible, disastrous, evil, and demonic dreams. Dreaming of snakes and reptiles--, not good--, you're captive.

You need to know what your dreams mean from a reputable biblical source or knowledgeable Christian minister. Seek out a reputable person, book, or website. Don't just look your dreams up on psychic or random websites. That will get you in worse trouble. And yes, there are spiritual attacks while you are sleeping.

The Kingdom of Heaven is like a man who sowed good seed in his field, but while men slept, his enemy came and sowed tares, (that's weeds), among the wheat, and went his way.

Yes, attacks happen at night. And if you haven't learned that, you won't get away with resisting God. Then you should, because at the Name of Jesus, every knee will bow. There will be a day of reckoning.

When is it?

I don't know. No one knows. But at the Name of Jesus, every knee should bow of those in heaven, and those on Earth and those under the Earth, And that every tongue should confess that Jesus Christ is Lord to the glory of God the Father.

The devil may be thinking that he can't get you *un*saved, but you might be just trying to get you bound and heavily yoked and burdened, so you don't live the abundant life that God has for you.

The devil wants to compromise you, if not fully, a bit at a time, a piece at a time. He just wants you to have a miserable life, and your testimony will be horrible. Your witness will be nonexistent, and we are called to be a witness in the Earth by our life, our lifestyle, by our words, by our actions and deeds.

But God will have respect unto you, and He will make covenant with you. He'll give you rain in due season, and make you a tree that bears fruit and allow the vintage that you have to minister to you until you sow next year. You won't suffer insufficiency or run out of anything. You're gonna have plenty of bread to eat, and you will dwell in your land safely. There'll be peace in your land.

Nobody will make you afraid. Nobody. God will get the evil beasts out of the land, and He will cause war not to come upon your land. And if you chase your enemies, they will run from you; they will be afraid of you.

I will have respect unto you. And make you fruitful and multiply you and establish my covenant with you. (Leviticus 26:9)

You will have more than enough, and not have to live hand-to-mouth. God says He will Tabernacle among you. Glory to God. And God says, **I will walk among you and be your God, and you shall be my people.**

God wants to Tabernacle with us. He wants to walk with us and be our God, and that we should be His people, the sheep of His pasture.

For I am the Lord your God, which brought you forth out of the land of Egypt, that you should not be their bondman. And I've broken the bands of your yoke and made you go upright.

God offers us freedom and deliverance only through God, only God. These are the things that come from respect, being respected by God and being in covenant with God, whereas the devil has been resisting God for centuries. And what he can expect for that is to burn in a lake of fire and brimstone forever, and ever, in eternal damnation, that is not made for us, that is not made for man.

Things Happen in Life

Revelation 18:10-13 thus: "Standing afar off for the fear of her torment, saying, Alas, alas, that great city Babylon, that mighty city! for in one hour is thy judgment come. And the merchants of the earth shall weep and mourn over her; for no man buyeth their merchandise any more.

The merchandise of gold, and silver, and precious stones, and of pearls, and fine linen, and purple, and silk, and scarlet, and all thyine wood, and all manner vessels of ivory, and all manner vessels of most precious wood, and of brass, and iron, and marble.

And cinnamon, and odours, and ointments, and frankincense, and wine, and oil, and fine flour, and wheat, and beasts, and sheep, and horses, and chariots, and slaves, and souls of men.

This is the stuff that Babylon is **selling**. Yet we are charged to possess our souls, and we need our whole souls. But **Babylon is trading in the souls of men.**

Why?

To capture you.

To steal your power.

To steal your glory, destiny.

Star virtues

To thwart your purpose for being here on Earth.

Without the soul, everybody will just be practically the same—, Stepford wives, zombies, robots. It is the soul that distinguishes between individuals. It is the soul that makes us powerful beings.

Only God can deliver any mind that is caged in a demonic trap. A person whose mind is demonically caged will never achieve his or her potential in life. A person whose emotions are caged and under the power of evil entities will not make sound decisions or reach purpose or destiny. A person whose will is out of their own control will make errors and mistakes and missteps constantly. You need your soul to conduct business and *occupy* until Jesus returns. You need your soul to also be whole to be effective in all your endeavors.

This is where we need others who will tell us the truth in love when we are in need of deliverance because we may not be ourselves or see ourselves. Worse, we may be so far into captivity and needing deliverance that we can't get out on our own.

Wilderness temptations of Jesus—was the devil trying to get Jesus' soul?

Satan tempting Jesus in the Wilderness: Was Satan trying to trick Jesus out of His soul? Was the devil trying to compromise Jesus' soul? Job was tested, but God said, **Don't kill him.**

Jesus' temptations follow three patterns that are common to all men. The first temptation concerns the *lust of the flesh*

(Matthew 4:3–4). Our Lord is hungry, and the devil tempts Him to convert stones into bread, but He replies with Scripture, quoting Deuteronomy 8:3.

When this first temptation came to Jesus, His *time* had not come yet. In order to turn stones to bread Jesus would have had to use magic or demonic power to make this happen, and that is a soul trade if a man does that.

The second temptation concerns the ***pride of life*** (Matthew 4:5–7), where the devil said to Jesus, Throw yourself down and angels will save you. Jesus didn't want to abuse power; He was never drunk with power. If you get drunk with power that proves that your soul is not mature enough to have that power. So, until your mind, will, intellect and emotions are mature, perhaps you don't need power yet. To cajole Jesus, here the devil uses Psalm 91:11–12, but the Lord replies again with Scripture to the contrary (Deuteronomy 6:16), stating that it is wrong for Him to abuse His own powers.

Jesus was never drunk with power as many humans can be. Your soul needs to be mature enough not to be drunk with power. Listen: Your will is matured. Your emotions are matured. Your intellect is matured, that is what a prospered soul looks like.

The third temptation concerns the *lust of the eyes* (Matthew 4:8–10), Jesus had asked God later on if the Cup of Sorrows could pass from Him—wouldn't any man ask that? If Jesus had let the devil give him control over all the kingdoms of the world, (Ephesians 2:2), which the devil already controlled, then Jesus would have to give allegiance to Satan and not to God.

Who in their right mind would want Satan as their father? Man doesn't think this all the way through when they want a shortcut to the top or to fame, or to wealth.

Jesus doesn't just know the Word; Jesus IS the Word and He replies to Satan, **"You shall worship the Lord your God and serve Him only."** That was a real smack in the face too, since Satan had been created as Lucifer as the worship leader in Heaven and had defected to try to become God, himself.

This is the place where humans get desperate, greedy, lustful, and maybe display their ignorance and stupidity. Humans think of success, fame, glory, wealth, sometimes even their flesh--, this is where the *risk* of soul trading comes in. Where people say STUPID things. Or souls are traded even when nothing is said but the transaction is IMPLIED.

CAREFUL!

When people say they would give anything, trade anything, give their first born--, don't say things like that.

Sometimes nothing is said or has to be said, it is understood that this goes with that. If you participate in a thing, you agree with it. As you see, desperation opposes patience. If we are to be anxious for nothing, then we should also not be desperate at any time. (Housewives, take note.)

In your patience possess ye your souls.
(Luke 21:19)

Jesus knew He was going to get the thing that God Promised Him anyway – so why rush it or force it? Be patient. Patience is not only a Fruit of the Spirit it is a what would Jesus do answer to any number of questions.

Jesus didn't come to Earth to save mankind to get a promotion; He was not self-serving in the least. Jesus came for us because of Love--, Love for the Father, and Love for us which the Father had given to Him. Getting something out of the deal is a manmade, flesh construct. When Jesus agreed to come to Earth to redeem mankind back to the Father Jesus was all Spirit and was pre-incarnate and not yet a man in flesh. If Jesus had come to get something out of the whole deal, He would have built a magnificent kingdom here on Earth and He would have milked it by living a long, long, time. Thirty years is not a long time to live, but Jesus' mission was done, so we see He came for the mission, and the mission, alone.

We don't try to get ahead of God; we don't try to get things out of season. We don't trade our gazillion-dollar soul for *things and stuff.*

In your patience, possess ye your souls.

Temptation to idol worship, idolatry, soul *trading, soul selling,* satanic worship for *things and stuff*—and for things and stuff, **right NOW**, can happen if we want it fast. The devil is showing you things so you can see it and make you want it. That tactic appeals to the pride of the eye.

The devil will find a way to put that thing right in your face. Whether it's a designer handbag or somebody else's spouse – whatever the thing is that you want, if it is illegal, out of bounds, or appeals to the flesh in a way that will eventually harm you, initiate you, indoctrinate, or compromise you, the devil will find a way to present or offer it to you.

Monitoring *spirits* in the Earth see what you watch, and they know what you are fascinated with or what you want or are lusting for. Even if you never say it out loud. Well, what do you know? Here comes that temptation right up to you. If you're very ignorant or self-centered and ungodly you may think, *Oh, my life is going great,* (until it's not). *Things I want just come to me.* OMG.

Seems like it's going great—until it's not. A fish thinks a worm is pretty tasty until he finds himself jerked out of water – out of his environment with no air to breathe. Lights out for that fish.

> May your whole spirit, soul and body be preserved blameless at the coming of our Lord Jesus.
> (1 Thessalonians 5:23)

The devil likes to tempt man to do some funky stuff just to see how low man will go so he can then go to God and blame man for the thing man just did that was so low. The devil goes to accuse man, with an evil petition to get a judgment against that man, which is permission from God to waste that man. That's what happened to Job.

The devil is putting sin traps, masked as *things and stuff* in your view and laying them at your feet. Please don't think that your life is going great because temptation after temptation is coming into your view, or into your life.

Conversely, God, the righteous parent is *telling you about what is going to be coming into your life,* to inspire your Faith. God is trying to inspire your faith while the devil is trying to inspire your eye, your flesh. God is loving you unconditionally, but requiring some soul growth before you get what you have asked Him for – even though the answers to our prayers from God are Yes, and Amen, so it doesn't destroy you. God requires soul growth **before** you get the something that God has promised you.

The devil may be bringing you some of the very things or something so close to the thing that God has for you, but the devil is bringing it out of season. Have you ever noticed the out of season fruit is very expensive and while it looks good on the outside, it is usually not tasty when you eat it?

What you get from the devil could be out of season because it's not ready to be presented to you yet, or consumed, and/or you are not ready for it, even though you want it and even though it looks good, on the outside, but will it turn bitter in your belly?

Men are more moved by the eye, by what they see more than women are. So, it is so it is SOOOOO it's probably much easier for the devil to tempt men. Especially since there are women everywhere whereas to tempt the average woman, you have to go *look for* an expensive handbag to buy.

Men might be easier to tempt when there are silly or desperate women who work for Satan and may not even realize that they work for him. They are working for Satan for free. They are getting nothing of value from the devil for allowing him to use them in ritual sex activities, but then one day they will find that they are in bondage to sin, and no longer free.

That thing offered to eye-candy-seeking men is most often SIN—it's fire, it's sin. Sometimes it doesn't look like sin but sometimes it does, but the average person may think that they can play with this *strange fire* and not be burned.

When a person finds him or herself in bondage to sin and they keep repeating the sin and can't stop that is a sign that their soul has been sold.

Can a man take fire in his bosom, And his clothes not be burned? Can one go upon hot coals, And his feet not be burned? So he that goeth in to his neighbour's wife; Whosoever toucheth her shall not be innocent.
(Proverbs 6:27-29)

Aside from the obvious burning by any kind of strange fire, the bondage of the sin is evident in the branding of that man or woman. They've been burned and an evil mark has been placed in them, or on them, like cattle, indicating that they are property of the devil. They are not supposed to be the devil's property, but they have partaken of the devil's wares so much that he has laid claim to them. That is the strange fire. That is the burn. And, that is the branding, the evil mark.

Multiple Sales

It's easier to be tempted, when you **want** to be tempted. When you pursue eye candy, adventure, excitement, FIRE, SIN. Especially if you're looking for it, it's really easy for the devil to tempt you. Especially if you're asking for it. I heard a married man once in a sigh-prayer that he just wanted something "*different*."

Who was he praying to?

Where in the Bible is that?

Drink waters out of your own cistern is what I read in my Bible. Be satisfied with the wife of your youth. That sighing man was soon divorced.

Whoever brought him *something different* also latched on to his soul. It wasn't God because God doesn't steal, kill, destroy, buy, or sell souls. Once that married man accepted something "*different*," he had sold his soul. His career has struggled since. Career and financial woes can be a sign of a sold soul.

Adulterous man who went into his neighbor's wife, sold his own soul. Sin sells souls.

When you sin, your spirit man will convict you, if you do not repent then you could spiral down in life because of it, selling and then destroying your own soul.

> For what does it profit a man to gain the
> whole world, and forfeit his soul?
> (Mark 8:36)

A person in the bondage of ritual sex cannot be satisfied with their own spouse and they must run the streets. In this way the idols in their souls have placed anti-marriage,

marriage failure, and poverty curses on them, enjoining them from being married or enjoying their marriage. Their souls are sold. If they are the ones who willingly sinned to get this bondage underway, they have sold their own souls.

> For thus saith the LORD, Ye have sold
> yourselves for nought; (Isaiah 52:3a)

So, a man or woman can sell themselves into slavery or bondage and not even realize it. They can sell themselves and not receive anything for it, that is unless you believe sex, in our current example is a reward.

A person can sell their soul multiple times, after all it is worth a gazillion dollars. A soul can be sold by others multiple times. This is possible if there are no walls of protection around you. If there is no roof on your house. If you are not saved. If you are saved but still carnal and sinning. An occultic or witchcraft person can turn you over as a candidate for stealing from, killing, or destroying. They may do this to save their own hide, or to get promotion in the underworld.

> Thus says the Lord GOD "Woe to the women who sew magic charms on their sleeves and make veils for the heads of people of very height to hunt souls! Will you hunt the souls of My people, and keep yourselves alive? (Ezekiel 13:18)

It was said in one family that a certain person in that family would sell anyone out, even their own grandmother. Why the family laughed about it is a mystery, other than people often can't clearly see the witchcraft that is right under their noses. Really, they've been desensitized to believe that their family members that they've been forced to grow up with are evil and can mean them no good at all. Especially since your parents keep telling you to get along with your siblings, and to love them.

But the Bible tells us this:

> Do not suppose that I have come to bring peace to the earth. I did not come to bring peace, but a sword. For I have come to turn a man against his father, a daughter against

her mother,
a daughter-in-law against her mother-in-
law— a man's enemies will be the
members of his own household. Anyone
who loves their father or mother more than
me is not worthy of me; anyone who loves
their son or daughter more than me is not
worthy of me. (Matthew 10: 34-27)

So the household witch or warlock in your family can sell any and all of you out at any time because he or she has both access and the same blood. If you are not saved, sanctified, set aside and prayed up, you can be a potential victim.

Here's a real example, a brother in a family always has money, his sisters don't. He sits as king of the family, and everyone comes to him when in financial need. The sisters are far more educated than he is, but he sits as king.

This brother has sold out his sisters' careers, virtues, stars. How do I know? The dream was had by one of the sisters years ago that he drove his car into the ocean. No, it wasn't an accident, he willfully drove his car into the ocean. The thing was the sister that had this dream was a passenger in the front seat, but as he drove into the ocean, she ended up standing on the sidewalk of that city, dry, without a drop of water on her as she watched him drive into the deep green water.

- Marine witchcraft, loose your hold on my life, right now, in the Name of Jesus.
- Anyone who has stolen from me and are offering to help me look for what *they* stole, let your power die, in the Name of Jesus.

If you're involved in astral projection, your soul is sold; there is no defense.

Weird dreams that won't stop – the soul has been sold multiple times.

Soul tied is when a person can not leave a thing, place, or person; they are stuck in time, so to speak, back when they were together, or were married, or loved one another. It could happen to both, or one may have moved forward, but the other hasn't. A tied soul is a sold soul. Did you sell it, or did the other person that you gave access to your soul do this to you? It could be either case.

If you have trouble saying, No, your soul is sold.

Out of Season

The devil doesn't care if you get things and stuff, he just wants you to get it out of turn, out of sequence, out of order, or out of season so it will compromise or destroy you.

Look at the following connections and their sequelae:

Abraham-Hagar-Ishmael. Abimelech gave Abraham the slave, Hagar. Isaac was the promise, but Abraham's wife, Sarah was also impatient, not possessing her soul in patience and handed Abraham that *apple*. That apple was Hagar. Abraham bit, that *apple*, and then later on the fruit of that biting bit Sarah, then

Abraham and since then a whole lot of other people.

God promised Abraham-Sarah-Isaac. And as you see the Promise came through Isaac, but impatience and unbelief created Ishmael.

The devil only offers you things that he can hook you with, and/or things that will destroy you, based on your inability to handle it – because your soul is not prospered. In this way the thing that would be a blessing when you get it from God is not a blessing from the devil; it is bait. It is custom-made bait designed to capture your soul.

If you are not ready, you are not ready, and this is why you don't yet have it from God. It doesn't mean you're never going to get what God has promised you. For the protection of your soul God might be the delay, or because of not being prospered in your soul yet, you might be the reason why it's taking so long.

Two different times Abraham said that Sarah was his sister because he didn't want to be killed. Sarah even agreed and told Abimelech that she was Abraham's sister. That could be another reason why it took so long for Isaac to get here—, *lying, yeah*, but also how can a child of Promise get here between a *brother and a sister*. *Ewww*!

How about this one?

Adam-Eve-Cain.

Obviously, God was pleased with Abel, but since Cain and Abel are mentioned by some scholars to be twins, Adam and Eve got a good one and a bad one. Cain committed the first murder, and the *spirit of Cain* seems to be in the Earth still, while Abel's blood is crying out from the ground. It should have been Adam-Eve-Abel, that would have been far more in line with what God was doing by creating a paradise and blessing man with life and putting him in that Garden.

Adam wasn't managing his house well and that takes soul prosperity. Eve, not prospered in her soul either, fell for the *okie doke* that the serpent was dropping, so she wasn't wise or prospered enough in her soul.

But Eve got busy, and I don't believe it was eating an apple, but that's my opinion. Abel belonged to God and to Adam, but that other one –, Cain, in my opinion was too much like the devil to even need a DNA test. (my opinion).

This may be too much for many, but if God made Adam and Eve and put them in the Garden and told them to be fruitful and multiply, wouldn't the devil want to get in on that? *Wouldn't he?* Especially since by Genesis 6 fallen angels were marrying or getting with the daughters of men. Have you ever thought of where they got the idea to do that? Have you ever thought about that? I think they got the idea from their own father, Satan.

Don't Lose It

How can a person lose their soul?

When they are dealing with people who collect or trade in souls. Do people who deal with the devil not realize that he is a collector of souls, and that he buys and sells souls? For example, you might want fame, the cost of that is your soul. You might want money, the cost of that is your soul. You might want this, that, or the other--, the cost is always your *gazillion-dollar* soul.

People who have become desperate or made themselves desperate will take out their gazillion dollar soul and put it on the counter to purchase something that is never *worth* a gazillion dollars. When people get greedy, lusty, jealous, or desperate, and they have either decided or let the devil tell them that money, things and stuff will satisfy the lack or the need they have, that is when they enter into devil deals. That is when they lose their souls; they sell their own souls.

If they hold power or position more dear than God, people, and protocol they are at risk of selling their soul. When they hold money more dear than people. When they celebrate their flesh and are not willing to lay it down—even for relationships. Ultimately when you put God either on a back burner or take Him off the stove altogether--, it's over *Bruh*.

- We are trading all day and all night, even in our sleep. Pray to the Lord that you are not using your soul to trade when if you are conducting business, you should use the world's creation—money to conduct business, not your soul.

Every day you're trading your life, your time, your blood, sweat, labor and toil for something. Don't trade your soul, however, for fleeting pleasure, or even out-of-season promises that God has made to you, but you just can't wait to be king. Don't trade it to gratify your immediate needs or wants.

Use your soul to worship, honor and serve God for Kingdom business and righteousness, & purpose, to maintain and prosper your soul. But do not use your soul in trade for Earth business.

Esau is a man who traded his soul for fleeting pleasure. He sold his birthright, which included not only material benefits, family inheritance, and spiritual blessings, for a bowl of soup. It says that he ate and drank and rose and went on his way (Genesis 25:34). He didn't give a second thought about what he had done. He did it, it felt good, and only much later did he come to regret it.

Much like the adulterous woman who wipes her mouth and goes on, even though she's made a soul trade. She and whomever she sinned with; the devil got their souls. Neither of them may realize it right now, after all they are basking in the afterglow of sin and believe they have been to nirvana and reached bliss.

Esau traded and the devil got in that contract. From then on Esau's life went further down. It seems that Esau did enjoy some wealth since he rejected Jacob's offer when Jacob wanted to give him cattle, but Esau made bad decisions, married Canaanite women, and became the father of the Edomites and further *unfavored* by God.

Again, I speak of the Truth in Love. When a person has lost or traded their soul—they may not even be aware of it, they just find that their life sucks and things are not working out well. Their souls need to be *called back* and healed completely through the divine intervention of the Lord Jesus Christ.

A person may decide to sell his own soul to the devil. You might be surprised how many people talk to the devil on a regular basis anyway. Wouldn't the devil talk back seeing that they have a ready customer and try to sell them something and at a huge mark up?

Behold, for your iniquities *have ye sold yourselves*, (Isaiah 50:1)

We don't know how many people have made verbal contracts with the devil, who would *"give anything for"*...

Guard your words. Hyperbole sounds like fun, but it can get you into a devil covenant that you may not even be aware that you made. Or you don't have spiritual intercession, prophets, pastors to pray for you.

People who would *give anything, left arm, right legs, first born* –, as said before none of this stuff is funny; it is serious, and it may be more real than you have previously thought. You've got to renounce those words, take them back, now!

Don't get it twisted, a person may not always *trade* their soul – they could be tricked out of it unless the Holy Spirit tells us.

What? Yup. That doesn't just happen in the movies.

Everyone you meet is not real and they may not even be what they appear to be. Some are on assignment from the enemy. Ever see a person who looks too good to be real... uh huh... spotlessly clean, and naturally good-looking. *You'd better ask God.* Any person having affairs with these so-called beautiful human beings--, better ASK God instead of assuming that what you wanted that day, that moment, right now just *presented itself to you*, like magic. Is a soul snatcher a real thing, spiritually speaking... better ask God. You need your whole soul.

Always be guarded when you are enticed to sin; once you sin anything can happen to you. *Come on, let's do it, it will be fun. Let's do it; nothing will happen to you. Come on, no one will know.* If someone wants you to sin more than anything they are more than likely a soul snatcher, a star hunter, or someone desiring to curse you and they want to make sure the curse will alight. We don't know What deals anyone has made with the devil either on purpose or if they have been tricked.

A third way of losing your soul is also by being unprotected spiritually and you get **nominated** by some evil entity or evil human agent to have your soul taken captive or stolen and you do nothing about it. This means you agree with what is coming down the pike for you. God will show you the devil's plans in a dream, for example, but if you don't understand the dream, don't know what the dream means, or do nothing about it--, specifically prayer treat it, then it means you agree with it and what the devil has planned for you will happen in your life.

Say it ain't so.

Wish I could, but it is so.

Soul Merchants

Soul traders of my father's house, soul traders of my mother's house, DIE, in the Name of Jesus.

Any sin in my life that is allowing the enemy to trade with my soul, enter into the Blood of Jesus, and die, in the Name of Jesus.

Any sin in my life that is making me a soul trader, and I am now handing souls over to the kingdom of darkness, let that power die, in the Name of Jesus.

Every power of the enemy that is using me as a soul trader, die, in the Name of Jesus.

Every strange fire that must be quenched, let it quench now, in the Name of Jesus.

Strange fire in the womb, quench now, in the Name of Jesus.

Strange fire in the body, quench now, in the Name of Jesus.

Strange fire in the head, quench now, in the Name of Jesus.

Strange fire in the hands, quench now, in the Name of Jesus.

Strange fire of witchcraft working evil in my body, die, in the Name of Jesus.

Any strange fire working for the enemy to bring reproach, disgrace, or shame to my name, Lord, let that fire quench now, in the Name of Jesus.

Strange fire in my life that is working for darkness, quench and die, in the Name of Jesus.

Cain turned Abel over to darkness as a sacrifice; Cain was a soul hunter. Any sin working in my life to turn me into a soul merchant, die, in the Name of Jesus.

Iniquities employed to sponsor the sale of my soul, die, in the Name of Jesus.

Any power from my family background seeking to make a shipwreck of my life and ministry, be destroyed by the Fire of God, in the Name of Jesus.

Any agent of Satan carrying my blood to kill me, Blood of Jesus, destroy them, in the Name of Jesus. *Amen.*

Love Bombed then Ghosted?

Have you been love-bombed, and then ghosted? Whoever is suspending love will sell you; they will sell your soul.

People who curse, love cursings, and use curse words are soul merchants.

Been sold out by ancestral sin or evil dedication. Evil foundation, family with occultic or witchcraft history, your soul may have been on the auction block before you ever had a soul, hundreds of years before you were ever born.

When we sin and then lead someone else into sin we are handing over their souls to darkness. Has your soul been sold?

Only Jesus can buy us back. Even if you sold yourself for nothing, Jesus will buy you back and without cost to you.

First thing, repent. Oh, you may think you didn't do anything, you're the victim. Yeah, right. The curse could not alight unless there was sin and then some iniquity due on your part, so repent.

Next forgive all who have ever offended you. *Why*? Because unforgiveness is a sin, a common sin, so you see you really do have something to repent for.

A soul can be sold and resold and resold, like a property with multiple liens on it. The more sin in your life, the more opportunities for your soul to be sold. When you sin, you sell your own soul to the devil. If you are in the bondage of sin or have iniquity on your head, anyone else who wants to nominate and sell your soul can do it more easily. And then there's the issue that your soul could have already been sold before you ever got to earth by evil dedication or bloodline ancestral iniquity which you just inherit by being born to the parents that you were born to.

Pray—

Whoever is about to sell my soul next, I'm in Christ and I cannot be sold; sell yourself, in the Name of Jesus.

Where I have gotten my soul sold consciously or unconsciously, sacrifice of Christ redeem my soul, in the Name of Jesus.

The need that has gotten my soul sold consciously and unconsciously to darkness, sacrifice of Christ meet the need and redeem my soul, in the Name of Jesus.

 Dark altars that supervised the sale of my soul, collapse, die and release my soul, by the power in the Blood of Jesus.

Family member turned agent of darkness that handed over my soul, let your power die and release my soul, in the Name of Jesus.

Bewitchment and enchantment at work to make merchandise of my soul, backfire in the Name of Jesus.

Ancestral debts owed by my ancestors that cannot be paid except I die, let the sacrifice of Christ settle the debts and redeem my soul, in the Name of Jesus. *Amen.*

The fight for your soul is complicated and many-faceted. Know that the struggle is real and seek more information and teaching on this.

Traded, Sold Souls

Every gathering of the wicked in my father's house, in my mother's house, in my place of work designed to put me to shame, scatter, in the Name of Jesus.

Time & space, cooperate with me and not with my enemies, in the Name of Jesus.

Whoever is invoking my name to hand me over to darkness, let your power die, in the Name of Jesus.

Every environmental bewitchment operating upon my life, come out and backfire, in the Name of Jesus.

Everything that is going on in my life only to break my fellowship with Heaven, backfire, in the Name of Jesus.

Who is selling my soul to meet their needs, let their agenda backfire, in the Name of Jesus.

Every curse operating upon my life and has handed me over to darkness, Blood of Jesus, break the Curse!

Whatever must be uncovered that I may move forward, let Heaven uncover it, in the Name of Jesus.

Whoever Heaven has separated me from but they will not be separated, let Heaven separate them from me by Force, in the Name of Jesus.

When Heaven has separated me from you, but you said you will not be separated from me, let the forces of Heaven separate you by Force.

Lord, put an end to all witchcraft troubling my soul and body, in the Name of Jesus. (Micah 5:12 NLT)

Hands of witchcraft laid on my head, laid on my body, die in the Name of Jesus.

Altars of the wicked in my father's house, altars of the wicked in my mother's house sponsoring the strange battles in my life, DIE, in the Name of Jesus.

The curse that got my soul sold to darkness, Blood of Jesus break the curse and let my soul be released, in the Name of Jesus.

My soul, let the Blood of Jesus redeem you from the battle of satanic invocation of jilted partners and lovers, in the Name of Jesus.

My soul, let the Blood of Jesus redeem you from the battle of satanic invocation of stalkers, known and unknown, in the Name of Jesus.

My soul, let the Blood of Jesus take you out of the register of those who must die by sickness, in the Name of Jesus.

My soul, let the Blood of Jesus take you out of the register of poverty, in the Name of Jesus.

My soul let the Blood of Jesus take you out of the register of failure, in the Name of Jesus.

Soul merchants, soul handlers using the basis of my location to trade with my soul, let your powers die, and release my soul, in the Name of Jesus.

Blood covenants allowing my soul to be traded, break and die, in the Name of Jesus.

Powers that have become evil invocators for my sake and are putting up my soul for sale, fall down, and die, in the Name of Jesus.

The sin serving the enemy to enslave and entrap me, die, in the Name of Jesus.

If where I live is making my soul able to be traded or handed over to darkness, O God arise and relocate me, in the Name of Jesus.

Better pray to God especially if your life looks anything like this:

- One step forward, two steps back.
- Tragedy supplants success all the time or more often than not.
- Your spouse is just not him or herself suddenly.
- Haven't been able to receive the Holy Spirit? Check your soul.
- Repetitive dreams where you are lost?
- Feeling lifeless like your energy has been drained out of you?
- Can't get your ex out of your mind?
- Soul tied--, big time.
- Wandering mind –can't focus. You can hardly make independent decisions anymore.
- Unexplained sicknesses.

Pray fervently; fight for your soul.

Careful of who touches your baby, or names your baby.

- False prophets and false prophetic words over me or my spouse or children, fall to the ground as dead works, in the Name of Jesus.

Pray seriously before you let anyone touch your baby, name your baby, or give you a prophecy that is not ordained by the pastor and/or body you worship in. You know that sweet little lady who confronts you in the bathroom or the parking lot??? Fake prophets can be anywhere. You have to renounce them, and the words spoken over you and your family. Every person, even in a church wasn't sent there by God.

There could be false preachers and false prophets, from the back of the house to the front. Better ask God.

I won't even talk about what people will do or try to do to maintain youth or to acquire money. We all need to cry out to God in prayers. We all need our whole souls to pray, to seek God to *occupy*, to maintain our work and purpose in the Earth and to intercede for the lost, both those who have never known God and those who may have backslidden.

We Sell Our Own Souls

We sell our own souls when we become a sinner. Worse, when we decide to sin, we also sign up for death. So your soul is not only sold, it is sold to Satan. Of course, God is not selling souls, so who would be looking to buy and trade in souls?

The body allows the soul to interface with the physical, it is why demons who don't have bodies, look for bodies to inhabit so they can interface in the physical.

The soul is the target. The soul is made in the image of God. The soul is needed and is milked for worship. People who do not intend to worship idols or idol gods somehow do. They participate in "fun" activities and festivals, for example not realizing that they are honoring pagan *gods*. In this the little g, *god* gets worship. Look at this, look at that, buy this, buy that, wear this, wear that, get a tattoo--, all these are ways that idol *gods* get worship.

Every time we worship an idol, we sell our souls.

After so much worship, idols claim ownership of a body. The strange fire causes a branding, and that claimed body is marked. The strange fire of sin burns, and it brands a spirit, a soul, and a body.

We should bear in our bodies the mark of the Lord Jesus Christ, but if we are serving strange *gods* and idols, we get branded by the kingdom of darkness.

Eve sold her own soul, then she sold Adam's—turned him over to darkness. Sin has a way of recruiting others to sin.

Signs of a Sold Soul

We mentioned the loss of humanity already.

Most often these types are living the image-driven life, concerned with appearance, status, money, et cetera. They are very superficial type folks. Many times, their conscience is seared or gone. *Seared--*, the result of the extreme heat of ***strange fire.***

They may be egomaniacal: they can make no mistakes; it's always some one else's fault. They are narcissistic, thinking they are better than other people. The narcissist thinks that they are more important than others, or really the **only** important one. They see others as pawns.

Signs of a sold soul:

- Confusion. Running from one place to another, such as one church to another. You can't get any peace.
- Your soul can be sold and resold and then sold again- multiple times. It is no respecter of persons or pedigree, or education, money. Nope.
- You're not yourself. It's hard to forgive others.

Parents can sell the souls of their children (evil dedication?)

We sell our own souls when we sin. You have sold your soul for nought.

The reason a soul can be sold so many times is because it is so valuable.

- Loss of respect for others and self.

- Will do anything for their desired goal, beauty, money, fame, celebrity, power.
- Impulse control is gone.
- They are users.
- Will sell out others and exploit them.
- You take delight in sabotaging others.
- The suffering of others delights you. Man, you've got issues.
- Hypocrite.
- Think you're the smartest person always; do not take wise counsel from others.
- *Spirits of competition* and *excessive competition* rules you.
- Petty and vengeful. Payback queen or king.
- It's about the big score. It's about the pleasure.
- This person can be double or even triple minded.
- Law breaker; will get what they want by any means necessary.
- Lost all values they allegedly used to have.

As bad as they treat others, they believe themselves the victim and they believe that they never get the good out of life that others get. Oh my!

Basically, any of the traits of the devil are the signs of a sold sou because people take on the nature and the personality--, no the *demonality* of the idols that they serve, are in connection with, or basically are married to.

As they say, in the natural when you've been married to someone for a long time you start to look alike. It's spiritual. If you're married to a demon, devil, idol, strange god, or devil long enough, you begin to look like them, that is act like them: UGLY. That's fleshy and ugly.

Substitution

Jesus was sold for 30 pieces of silver, the price of a slave, (Matthew 26). Since Jesus has been sold, He is then a substituted sacrifice for us. We can sell ourselves into bondage, that is, the bondage of sin, but we don't have to do this.

We can sell our own souls to the devil in trade for something temporal here on Earth; but we should not do that, and we don't have to do that.

My God shall supply all my needs according to His riches in Glory by Christ Jesus.

Jesus not only took on the sin of the world, but He also allowed Himself to be sold so w**e do not have to be sold again.** Joseph was sold by force. Slaves are taken by force. Jesus chose to save us by substitution, not by force but by choice.

We have been *bought back* by the Lord's sacrifice.

Lord, Redeem My Soul

But God will redeem my soul from the
power of the grave: for he shall receive me.
Selah. (Psalm 49:15)

They that trust in their wealth, and boast
themselves in the multitude of their riches;
None of them can by any means redeem his
brother, nor give to God a ransom for him:
(For the redemption of their soul is precious,
and it ceaseth for ever:)

But God will redeem my soul from the
power of the grave: for he shall receive me.
Selah. (Psalm 49:15)

Man can turn another man over to
death, to hell, to the grave, to captivity to
bondage, but he can't get him back; he cannot

redeem him. He can sell a man but can't buy him back.

When we mortgage our souls, we have not the power to buy ourselves back, or buy our way out of captivity and bondage. Yes, we can pray for our friends and for whomever the Lord puts on our heart to get them out of bondage, yokes, and captivity, but we, ourselves cannot bring a person out. It is by the Lord Jesus Christ, by the power of the Holy Spirit and by the mighty angels of God are any of us rescued from hell and captivity.

You would even cast lots for the fatherless and barter away your friend. (Job 5:27)

You'd better think long an hard before turning a soul over to the devil, to captivity, to death, hell, or the grave, because you cannot go get them again with a, *Nevermind*, or *I was just kidding.* When a person is in the devil's clutches, only the power of God, His Christ or the Holy Spirit can get them out of hell. Think again before you tell someone to go to h3ll, because there is such power in our words.

Jesus warned us to forgive even 70 x 7 because the consequences are **<u>very serious</u>**.

If you forgive anyone's sins, they are forgiven. If you do not forgive them, they are not forgiven. (John 20:23)

Not only is this forgiveness reciprocal, as in the Lord's prayer, but we are aspiring to be like Christ, therefore, if He would forgive, shouldn't we also, instead of condemning a person to hell and damnation, especially for some childish reason? *What reason?* Oh, I don't know, they cut you off on the highway, or took the parking space you were waiting for at the mall. Of course, there could be more serious reasons, but I give those to make you aware that you have power.

A third reason to forgive is that if God can't trust you with power, then you just won't have any power. It's why your prayers may not be answered because of unforgiveness because **power** was withdrawn from you because you are a danger with it, or you abuse power.

Prayers for Soul Freedom

Every unprofitable oath I made consciously or unconsciously in the spiritual world that is now affecting my life negatively, break in the Name of Jesus.

Soul merchants, soul handlers, using the basis of my location to trade with my soul, let your power die, and release my soul, in the Name of Jesus.

Blood covenants allowing my soul to be traded, break and die by the power in the Blood of Jesus.

The sin serving the enemy to enslave and entrap me, die, in the Name of Jesus.

If where I live is making my soul able to be traded, or handed over to darkness, O God arise, and relocate me, in the Name of Jesus.

You evil soul traders, release your captive today, in the Name of Jesus.

Lord, search the land of the living and the dead and gather every fragmented part of my soul and put me back together now, in Jesus' Name.

Oh Lord, restore my body, soul and spirit to the original perfect one you made for me, in Jesus' Name.

The law of the Lord is perfect, *restoring the soul*, The testimony of the Lord is sure, making wise the simple. Psalm 19:7

Every trauma that my soul has suffered, DIE out of my life, in the Name of Jesus.

Any demonic power that is using my soul as a residence, Fire of the Holy Spirit, enter my soul and burn those powers down, in the Name of Jesus.

Every battle that has swallowed my destiny, vomit my destiny, in the Name of Jesus.

Every battle that is satanic, demonic or witchcraft, let that battle DIE, in the Name of Jesus.

Soul traders of my father's house, DIE, in the Name of Jesus.

Soul traders of my mother's house, DIE, in the Name of Jesus.

Every sin in my life that is allowing the enemy to trade with my soul, enter into the Blood of Jesus, and DIE, in the Name of Jesus.

… will you hunt the souls of my people…
Ezekiel 13:18

Any sin in my life that is making me into a soul trader or a soul handler, let that sin DIE, in the Name of Jesus.

Every power of the enemy using me as a soul trader, die, in the Name of Jesus.

Whoever is carrying my blood and they are trading with my soul, let their power die, in the Name of Jesus.

My iniquities employed to sell my soul, take the Blood of Jesus, and die, in the Name of Jesus.

Who is about to sell my soul next, sell yourself, I am in Christ, in the Name of Jesus.

Where I have gotten my soul sold consciously or unconsciously, Blood of Jesus, redeem my soul, in the Name of Jesus.

The need that has gotten my soul sold consciously and unconsciously to darkness, sacrifice of Christ meet the need, and redeem my soul, in the Name of Jesus.

Dark altars that supervised the sale of my soul, collapse, die, and release my soul, by the power in the Blood of Jesus.

Family member turned agent of darkness that handed over my soul, let your power die and release my soul, in the Name of Jesus.

Bewitchment and enchantment at work to make merchandise of my soul, backfire, in the Name of Jesus.

Ancestral debts owed by my ancestors that cannot be paid, except I die, let the sacrifice of Christ settle the debts and redeem my soul, in the Name of Jesus.

Every gathering of the wicked in my father's house, in my mother's house, in my place of work designed to put me to shame, scatter, in the Name of Jesus.

Whoever is invoking my name to hand me over to darkness and punishment, let that power die, in the Name of Jesus.

Love of God in Christ Jesus, thank you.

Lord, forgive us for idolatry which breaks the fellowship with God.

Who is selling my soul to meet their needs, let their agenda backfire, in the Name of Jesus.

Who is selling my soul for promotion in the dark kingdom, let your agenda backfire, in the Name of Jesus.

Who is selling my soul for wealth, let your plan backfire, in the Name of Jesus.

Who is selling my soul for revenge and hatred, let your evil plots backfire in your face, in the Name of Jesus.

Who is selling my soul because of hatred, resentment, jealousy, greed, or any work of the flesh, let every sale backfire. Lord, preclude the sale, preclude the sale, in the Name of Jesus.

Every curse operating upon my life and has handed me over to darkness, Blood of Jesus, break the curse, in the Name of Jesus.

Whoever Heaven has separated me from, but they don't want to be separated from me, forces of Heaven, separate you by Force in the Name of Jesus.

Whoever is soul tied to me and won't let me go, the Lord put a Sword between you and me, in the Name of Jesus.

Weird dreams of soul captivity, I cancel you by the Blood of Jesus and let your evil against me be reversed, in the Name of Jesus.

Lord, I release everyone that I have been holding offense against, in the Name of Jesus.

Lord, I forgive all who have offended me, in the Name of Jesus.

Every mark on my body designed to capture my soul, become powerless, in the Name of Jesus.

Any scratch on my body designed to capture my soul, become powerless, in the Name of Jesus

Those cursing me day or night, or day and night, let your curses backfire, in the Name of Jesus.

Enemies in my household, let your power die, in the Name of Jesus.

Mercy of God in Christ, have Mercy on me and work forgiveness in my soul, in the Name of Jesus.

My Father, put an end to all witchcraft troubling my soul, in the Name of Jesus.

Hands with witchcraft laid on my head, laid on my body, DIE, in the Name of Jesus.

Altars of the wicked in my father's house, altars of the wicked in my mother's house sponsoring the battles in my life, DIE, in the Name of Jesus.

Bhe curse that got my soul sold to darkness blood of Jesus break the curse, break the evil covenant that allows the curse, and let my soul be released, in the Name of Jesus.

My soul, let the Blood of Jesus redeem you from the battle of satanic invocators, in the Name of Jesus.

My soul, let the Blood of Jesus redeem you from the battle of satanic invocation of jilted partners and lovers, in the Name of Jesus.

My soul, let the Blood of Jesus redeem you from the battle of satanic, occultic, witchcraft, astral projecting *spirit spouses*, in the Name of Jesus.

My soul, let the Blood of Jesus take you out of the register of those that must die by sickness, in the Name of Jesus.

Soul merchants, soul handlers, using my location to trade with my soul, let your power die, and release my soul, in the Name of Jesus.

Blood covenants allowing my soul to be traded, break and die by the power in the Blood of Jesus.

The sin serving the enemy to enslave and entrap me, die in the Name of Jesus.

If where I live is making my soul able to be traded, or handed over to darkness, O God arise, and relocate me, in the Name of Jesus.

Lord, let my imagination receive deliverance now, in the Name of Jesus.

Lord, block the imagination of any person who imagines and invokes evil over my life, in the Name of Jesus.

I know my Redeemer lives: Jesus Christ, the soul redeemer, redeem my soul today, in the Name of Jesus.

Jesus Christ the soul healer, heal my soul today, in the Name of Jesus.

He restores my soul: Jesus Christ the soul restorer, restore my soul today, in the Name of Jesus.

Dear Reader

Thank you for acquiring and reading this book. If your soul has been sold, may the Lord buy it back as He has promised. May you walk upright and blameless before Him in the future that your soul may never be sold again.

In the Name of Jesus,

Amen.

Dr. Marlene Miles

Other books by this author

AK: The Adventures of the Agape Kid

AMONG SOME THIEVES

Ancestral Powers https://a.co/d/9prTyFf

Backstabbers https://a.co/d/gi8iBxf

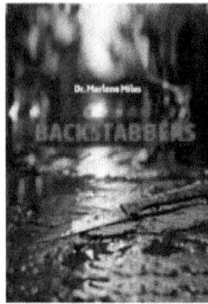

Barrenness, *Prayers Against*
https://a.co/d/feUltIs

Battlefield of Marriage, *The*

Blindsided: *Has the Old Man Bewitched You?* https://a.co/d/5O2fLLR

Break Free from Collective Captivity

Casting Down Imaginations

Churchzilla, The Wanna-Be, Supposed-to-be Bride of Christ

Curses of Blind Men

Demonic Cobwebs (prayerbook)

Demonic Time Bombs

Demons Hate Questions

Devil Loves Trauma, *The*

Devil Weapons: Unforgiveness, Bitterness,...

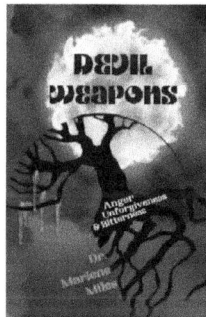

The Devourers: Thieves of Darkness 2

Do Not Swear by the Moon

Don't Refuse Me, Lord (4 book series)

https://a.co/d/idP34LG

Dream Defilement

The Emptiers: *Thieves of Darkness, 1*
https://a.co/d/5I4n5mc

Evil Touch

Failed Assignment

Fantasy Spirit Spouse
https://a.co/d/hW7oYbX

FAT Demons (The): *Breaking Demonic Curses*

The Fold (5-book series)

- The Fold (Book 1)
- Name Your Seed (Book 2)
- The Poor Attitudes of Money (3)
- Do Not Orphan Your Seed (4)
- For the Sake of the Gospel (5)
- My Sowing Journal

Gang Ups: Touch Not God's Anointed

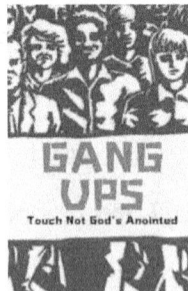

got HEALING? Verses for Life

got LOVE? Verses for Life

got HOPE? Verses for Life

got money? https://a.co/d/g2av41N

How to Dental Assist

How to Dental Assist2: Be Productive, Not Wasteful

I Take It Back

Legacy

Let Me Have A Dollar's Worth https://a.co/d/h8F8XgE

Level the Playing Field

Living for the NOW of God

Lose My Location https://a.co/d/crD6mV9

Man Safari, *The*

Marriage Ed. Rules of Engagement & Marriage

Made Perfect in Love

Money Hunters: Beware of Those

Money on the Altar https://a.co/d/4EqJ2Nr

Mulberry Tree https://a.co/d/9nR9rRb

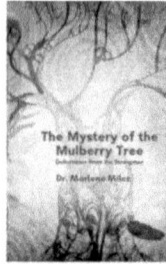

Motherboard (The) - *Soul Prosperity Series*

Name Your Seed

Occupy: *Until I Return*

Plantation Souls

Players Gonna Play

Power Money: Nine Times the Tithe

https://a.co/d/gRt41gy

The Power of Wealth *(forthcoming)*

Powers Above

The Robe, Part 1, The Lessons of Joseph

The Robe, Part II, The Lessons of Joseph

Seasons of Grief

Seasons of Waiting

Seasons of War

Second Marriage, Third~~, *Any Marriage*

https://a.co/d/6m6GN4N

Sift You Like Wheat

Six Men Short: What Has Happened to all the Men?

Soul Prosperity soul prosperity series 3

https://a.co/d/5p8YvCN

Souls Captivity soul prosperity series 2

The Spirit of Poverty

StarStruck

SUNBLOCK

The Swallowers: *Thieves of Darkness,* 3

Take It Back

This Is NOT That: How to Keep Demons from Coming at You

Time Is of the Essence

Too Many Wives: *Why You Have Lady Problems*

Tormenting Spirits https://a.co/d/dAogEJf

Toxic Souls

Triangular Power *(series)*

- Powers Above
- SUNBLOCK
- Do Not Swear by the Moon
- STARSTRUCK

Uncontested Doom

Unguarded Hours, *The*

Unseen Life, *The* (forthcoming)

Upgrade: How to Get Out of Survival Mode

- Toxic Souls (Book 2 of series)
- Legacy (Book 3 of series)

The Wasters: *Thieves of Darkness*, Bk 2
https://a.co/d/bUvI9Jo

What Have You to Declare? What Do You Have With You from Where You've Been?

When I Was A Child, *I Prayed As a Child*

When the Devourer is Rebuked

https://a.co/d/1HVv8oq

The Wilderness Romance *(series)* This series is about conducting a Godly relationship and marriage with someone who is a Wilderness person. It is about how to recognize it and navigate through it. These books are about how not to get caught up in such.

- *The Social Wilderness*
- *The Sexual Wilderness*
- *The Spiritual Wilderness*

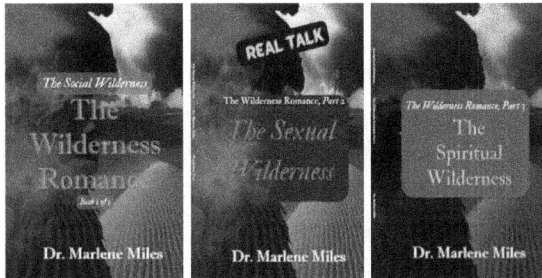

Other Series

The Fold (a series on Godly finances)
https://a.co/d/4hz3unj

Soul Prosperity Series https://a.co/d/bz2M42q

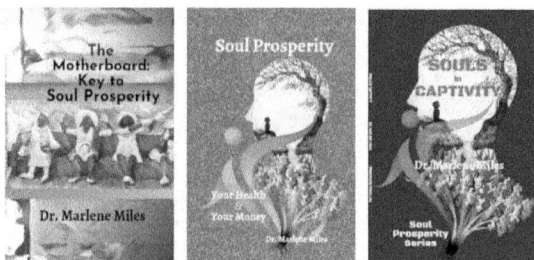

Spirit Spouse books

https://a.co/d/9VehDSo

https://a.co/d/97sKOwm

Thieves of Darkness series

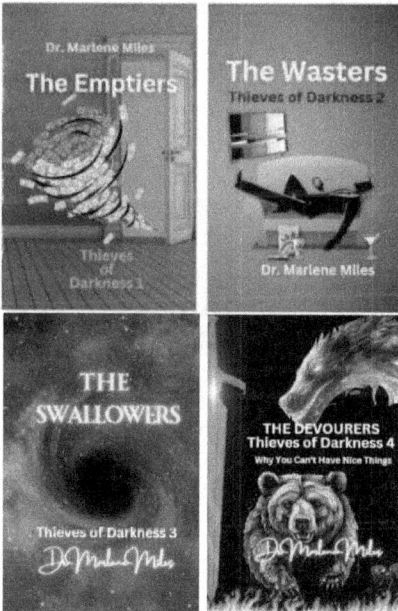

Triangular Powers https://a.co/d/aUCjAWC

Upgrade (series) *How to Get Out of Survival Mode*
https://a.co/d/aTERhXO

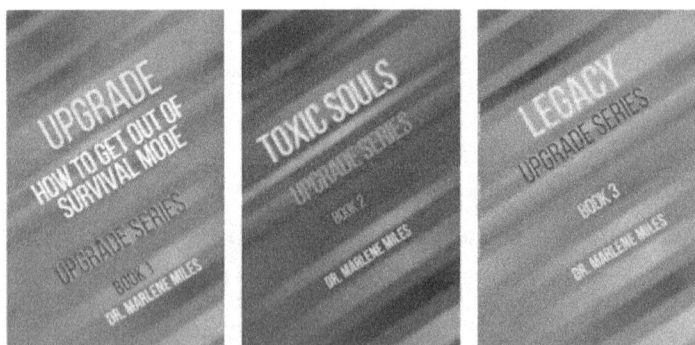

Prayer books by this author

While most books by this author have prayer points either throughout the book or at the end, there are some books that are only prayers. You just open up the book and pray. They are listed below:

Prayers Against Barrenness: *For Success in Business and Life*

Fruit of the Womb: *Prayers Against Barrenness*

Beauty Curses, *Warfare Prayers Against*
https://a.co/d/5Xlc2OM

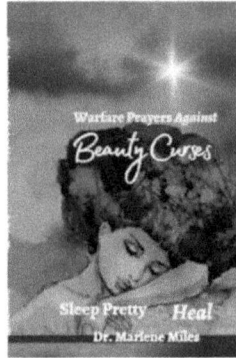

Courts of Marriage: Prayers for Marriage in the Courts of Heaven *(prayerbook)*
https://a.co/d/cNAdgAq

Courtroom Warfare @ Midnight *(prayerbook)*
https://a.co/d/5fc7Qdp

Demonic Cobwebs *(prayerbook)* https://a.co/d/fp9Oa2H

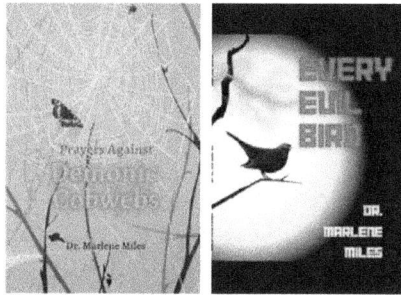

Every Evil Bird https://a.co/d/hF1kh1O

Gates of Thanksgiving

Spirits of Death, Hell & the Grave, Pass Over Me and My House

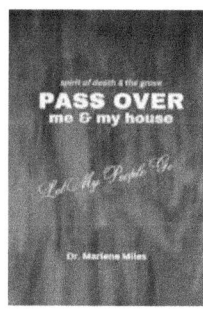

Throne of Grace: Courtroom Prayer

https://a.co/d/fNMxcM9

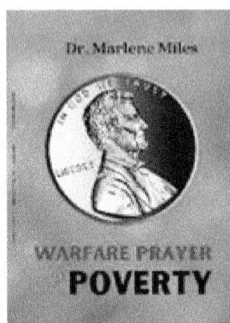

Warfare Prayer Against Poverty
https://a.co/d/bZ61lYu